A Call To America

Nancy Jesudass

Come to the Fire Publishing
Kansas City, Missouri

A Call To America
Copyright © 2016 Come to the Fire Publishing
Published by Come to the Fire
PO Box 480052
Kansas City, MO 64148
cometothefire.org
All rights reserved.

Library of Congress Cataloging in Publication Data:
ISBN 978-0-9905903-4-7
Printed in the United States of America

Table of Contents

Introduction 5

Chapter 1
Why I Love America..7

Chapter 2
Who Will Intercede for America? 8

Chapter 3
The Power of Intercessory Prayer...................................11

Chapter 4
How Big Is Your Burden? 13

Chapter 5
Will You Repent with Me? 17

Chapter 6
The Dream that Intensified My Burden 18

Chapter 7
For Such a Time as This 23

Chapter 8
What Will You Do with This Message?............................29

Introduction

In 1995 Nancy Jesudass heard Bill Bright challenge at the Los Angeles Prayer and Fasting to fast 40 days for revival in America. Her heart was stirred, but would her 90-pound frame survive 40 days with no food? Her doctor told her, "If you lose 20 pounds, you might die." Despite her fear, Nancy's heart was so burdened she entered the fast. She lost 20 pounds, but she gained an even deeper burden for our nation. The Lord led her to fast similarly additional years.

Five days a week I pray with Nancy. This morning was as many other mornings. "The Lord woke me up at 3:00 this morning, and my heart is burning for America with the burden that is on God's heart," she shared. One Friday on our way to the prayer room, we saw a group of children, and she began to weep. "They're going into exile," she said, referring to what God revealed to her in a dream described in this book.

This book is taken from talks Nancy gave pleading with people to become intercessors. After she spoke at the Come to the Fire conference, women emailed of their increased desire to intercede. They wrote:

"When Nancy Jesudass led us in an intercessory prayer, I felt an overwhelming burden." Another wrote, "I am challenged to keep the Lord's charge to pray without ceasing."

If Keith Green's words describe how you often feel, this book can bring a fresh burden for America.

My eyes are dry,
My faith is old.
My heart is hard,
My prayers are cold.

As you read, may Nancy's burdened prayer become yours: "Oh, how can I give you up, America? How can I bear to see the disaster fall on my people?"

Let us cry out for the future of the nation to our Father who is the "forgiving God, gracious and compassionate, slow to anger and abounding in love" (Nehemiah 9:17).

Aletha Hinthorn
Director, Come to the Fire

CHAPTER 1

Why I Love America

I owe my life to you. Yes, I owe Americans my life. I would like to tell you why.

One day over 100 years ago, a young man was wandering in the streets of Hanoi, North Vietnam, looking for a way to commit suicide. At that moment, an American missionary "happened" to appear and offered him a gospel tract. This young man had no interest in the tract but politely tucked it in his pocket without any intention of reading it.

The man had been forced by his parents to marry a woman he didn't love. He was addicted to opium and would go straight to an opium den after work, heading home around midnight. For about two years, that was his daily routine.

One evening in the opium den, the gospel tract fell out of his pocket. He picked it up and casually read it to pass time. The gospel message captured his heart to such an extent that he began looking for a local church to inquire more about Jesus. With the help of a pastor, this young man became a follower of Jesus and never returned to opium. He began a new life, seeking to love his wife as Christ loves the Church. Eventually he led his wife and all his children to Jesus. I was one of his eight children.

Thousands like my father were saved because of the love, fervent prayers, and sacrifices of Christians who took the gospel to Vietnam. My father became a serious follower of Jesus and a man of prayer. He was discipled by American missionaries and served the Lord wholeheartedly until he died at age 49. At that time I was 11 years old.

Likewise, missionaries taught me, discipled me, challenged me, and supported me financially, sending me to the Philippines and to the United States. Many Vietnamese have given their lives to full-time Christian service because of Christians from this great nation. I owe my life to them.

CHAPTER 2

Who Will Intercede for America?

I came to America from Vietnam in 1970 admiring the glory
of God upon this great nation. I rejoiced and enjoyed
America's many blessings.

However, as years passed, especially in the late 80's, I began
to notice America's moral decay and the spiritual downfall
slowly gripping this lovely land. I grieved deeply and shed many
tears as I painfully watched its decline.

One day in early 1991, while praying and walking, suddenly I
heard a voice, not audible but loud and clear, from within me.
"Nancy, are you willing to give up your part-time job and your
church activities to go into full-time intercession? I'm calling
you to be an intercessor, especially focused on revival in
America. Are you willing?"

I stood in awe of God's presence; I was speechless. I felt so
utterly unworthy. God's voice sounded so clear and so dear.

When I arrived home, I was still enjoying God's presence. I
said, "Yes, Lord, may it be to me as You have said." This was
Mary's response when the angel Gabriel visited her.

Since receiving that call more than 20 years ago, I have
prayed earnestly for our nation's revival. Sometimes I pray for
hours and hours for lost souls to come to Christ because our God
is the God of the Nations. When I find myself groaning in prayer,
it is Jesus travailing through me.

In January of 1998, God called me to a 40-day fast, drinking
only water and one glass of clear juice each day.

A year later, the Lord called me to fast again for 40 days in
the same manner but in two periods of 20 days at a time. Again, I
obeyed His voice.

The next year, He called me to fast for another 40 days in the
same manner but this time in four separate segments of ten
days at a time. Again, I obeyed.

During each fast I experienced God's heart crying through
me for this nation to repent, beginning with the house of God.
The more I cried through those years, the more I saw this nation
get worse and worse with little repentance.

In 2001 after 9/11, I said to God, "O Lord, this time we'll surely humble ourselves before you and repent."

And yes, there was some repentance, but it seemed to last for a short while. America's repentance was similar to what the prophet Hosea said to the Israelites: "Your love is like the morning mist, like the early dew that disappears" (Hosea 6:4).

I wondered why God might be delaying His answers to our prayers.

I realized God's stubborn love does not leave us alone. He pursues us until we respond to Him.

In the book of Judges and throughout the Old Testament we read, "Once again the Israelites did evil in the eyes of the Lord . . . Again the Israelites cried out to the Lord, and He gave them a deliverer" (Judges 3:12, 15).

God is ready to deliver us if we cry out to Him in brokenness and repentance.

One night in a dream I saw a long line of teenagers, and suddenly I became fully awake. I wondered what this meant.

The words came to me, "These young ones are going into exile."

"Exile?" I questioned.

And the voice repeated, "Yes, they are sent into exile every day." I thought about the word "exile." This is like God's people in the Old Testament when they continued in their sins and no longer cried out to God. They chose to trust in their own wisdom and knowledge and so were sent to Babylon to live in exile as captives under the rule of the ungodly.

I could not sleep any longer. I began to cry out to God for His mercy, His intervention, and His forgiveness. We have consciously or unconsciously allowed these young ones to suffer and to go astray. "My children have no future because the enemy has conquered us" (Lamentations 1:16 NLT).

The glory of God is no longer upon us. The nations around us seem to ask, "Where is your God?"

Within my spirit I can hear the lost around me crying out to us, the church, like the people of Nineveh cried out to Jonah: "How can you sleep? Get up and call on your God. Maybe He will take notice of us, and we will not perish" (Jonah 1:6). The Bible says that when the people in Nineveh cried to the Lord, the Lord saved that wicked nation because of their humility and repentant hearts.

Today, will you consider your Savior who prostrated Himself before God crying out for you and me? Jesus "offered up prayers and petitions with loud cries and tears" to God.

Today, God is still calling. "If my people, who are called by My Name, will humble themselves and pray and seek my face and turn from their wicked ways, then will I hear from heaven and will forgive their sin and will heal their land" (2 Chronicles 7:14).

The call to intercede, to pray on behalf of others, is a high calling. God is calling us to join Jesus as His intercessors on earth. God has intercession in heaven, and He must have intercession on earth so that His Kingdom may come and His will be done on earth as it is in heaven. Without the constant, fervent prayer in heaven and on earth, all our labor for the Gospel would be in vain.

"Now my eyes will be open and my ears attentive to the prayers offered in this place. I have chosen and consecrated this temple so that my Name may be there forever. My eyes and my heart will always be there" (2 Chronicles 7:15-16).

CHAPTER 3

The Power of Intercessory Prayer

Intercession is sweet communion with the LORD, yet it is also spiritual warfare.

Numbers 16 gives an example. Korah, one of Moses' leaders, formed a group of followers to rebel against Moses. In response, God's anger blazed against Korah's men. He sent a plague that caused 14,700 men to be swallowed by the earth.

You can imagine the terror—thousands of people in the camp screaming to Moses to call upon Aaron, his priest, to pray on their behalf.

"Then Moses said to Aaron, 'Take your censer and put incense in it, along with fire from the altar, and hurry to the assembly to make atonement for them. Wrath has come out from the LORD; the plague has started" (Numbers 16:46). With the fire from the altar, Aaron went through the camp, purified the people and made them right with God.

"Aaron stood between the living and the dead, and the plague stopped" (vs. 48).

You and I are made to be holy priests like Aaron who had the authority to intercede. It is more than a privilege—it is our responsibility. We are called to stand in the gap between the living and the dead. May God help us take our priesthood seriously.

God is calling to us, "Wake up, wake up, O Zion. Clothe yourself with strength" (Isaiah 52:1 NLT).

God longs to hear our voices and to meet with us face to face at the feet of Jesus. In Song of Songs 2:3, 14, God is saying: "Arise, come, my darling, my beautiful one, come with me . . . show me your face, let me hear your voice for your voice is sweet, your face is lovely."

When God called for intercessors, He asked why no one answered when He called. "Is it because I have no power to rescue? No, that is not the reason. For I can speak to the sea and make it dry. I can turn rivers into deserts and cover them with dying fish" (Isaiah 50:2).

Our compassionate, powerful God is ready to rescue those afflicted ones. They need someone to cry out to God on their behalf.

Let us stand in the gap for our nation as God's holy priests. (1 Peter 2:5) Let us intensely cry out to God like Moses and Aaron to save our people from the wrath of God. The Lord calls to us: "Return to me with all your heart, with fasting, weeping and mourning. Rend your heart and not your clothes. Return to the LORD your God for He is gracious and compassionate, slow to anger and abounding in love, and He relents from sending calamity" (Joel 2:12-13).

In 1 Samuel 12:23 the prophet said, "As for me, far be it from me that I should sin against the LORD by failing to pray for you."

"Lift up your voice with a shout, lift it up, do not be afraid" (Isaiah 40:9). To be an intercessor, all you need is a desire to obey and a heart willing to respond. Are you willing to respond to God's calling?

CHAPTER 4

How Big Is Your Burden?

Revivalist Dr. Ronnie Floyd made this statement: "Revival begins with a burden. How big is your burden?"

God gave the prophet Jeremiah a burden. God told him that Nebuchadnezzar, king of Babylon, would come and destroy the temple in Jerusalem and take the king of Judah and the people to Babylon as exiles. God said they must submit themselves to King Nebuchadnezzar.

Prophet Jeremiah went through tremendous sufferings for carrying God's message to His people. Both king and people rebelled. Jeremiah said, "I was like a lamb being led to the slaughter" (Jeremiah 11:19).

Jeremiah wept day and night over the people's sins. He said, "Streams of tears flow from my eyes because my people are destroyed" (Lamentations 3:48).

The more I read Jeremiah and Lamentations, the more I identify America with Israel. My heart burns within me. "Since my people are crushed, I am crushed" (Jeremiah 8:21).

Leonard Ravenhill, in his book *America Is too Young to Die*, said, "What is it that is missing from our churches? To use the Old Testament term, it is the burden of the Lord. One of the tragedies of the hour is that the voice of the prophet is no longer heard in the land. Where is the lamenting for the lost? Jeremiah's concern for his people caused him to weep day and night."

Jeremiah pleaded for his people: "Arise, cry out in the night as the watches of the night begin; pour out your heart like water in the presence of the Lord. Lift up your hands to Him for the lives of your children who faint from hunger at the head of every street" (Lamentations 2:19).

The prophet urges us to weep and cry for our nation today like he did for his own. "Cry aloud before the Lord...let your tears flow like a river day and night" (Lamentations 2:18 NLT).

"The Lord has withdrawn His protection as the enemy attacks" (Lamentations 2:3 NLT). Today our nation is like an open wound.

Are we concerned about what God is concerned about? Does what breaks the heart of God break our hearts?

Shall we just keep watching our nation fall until it totally collapses just as the Twin Towers were dashed to the ground in 2001? Isaiah stated, "So he poured out on them his burning anger, the violence of war. It enveloped them in flames, yet they did not understand; it consumed them, but they did not take it to heart" (42:25).

Dr. Kinlaw, in his book *The Mind of Christ*, wrote, "Apart from the Holy Spirit, you and I are too self-centered ever to care about anyone other than ourselves. If that burden for the lost ever stirs up within us, it did not start with us. It is the work of the Spirit of Jesus saying: 'Will you help me bear My burden?' If we say 'Yes' to Him and take that burden into our hearts, we will find ourselves doing what Paul talked about when he spoke of entering into the sufferings of Christ."

During the year 1777, when the United States was in conflict with Great Britain, a congressman asked John Adams if they would win the war. Adams answered, "Yes, if we fear God and repent of our sins."

Oh, may God help us. We must bring this nation back to God at any cost. We must save the future generations. If we fail to repent, we will lose our future generations to more broken families, pornography, violence, immorality and sodomization. America will no longer be great among the nations. In fact, she may have to go through humiliation as other great empires in the past did.

However, repentance of the church will result in revitalization, evangelism, missions and final preparation for the second coming of our Lord and Savior Jesus Christ. Repentance brings hope for the nations.

Listen to the agony of God's heart through the prophet Hosea (11:8 NLT): "Oh, how can I give you up Israel? How can I let you go? [America] How can I destroy you? My heart is torn within me and my compassion overflows."

Hear the prophet Jeremiah lamenting: "Rise during the night and cry out" (Lamentations 2:19).

And hear Paul crying to churches, "Time is running out. Wake up" (Romans 13:11 NLT).

Finally, hear Jesus' earnest voice to the Church and also to us: "Wake up. Strengthen what remains and is about to die, for I have not found your deeds complete in the sight of my God. Remember, therefore, what you have received and heard. Obey and repent" (Revelation 3:2-3).

God has expressed His deep longing to revive us as a nation through the prophets in the Bible. "I'll pour out water on the thirsty land, and streams on the dry ground; I will pour out my Spirit on your offspring and my blessing on your descendants" (Isaiah 44:3).

Revival begins with a burden, and the burden must begin with the people of God. Is now not the time for us to wake up from our slumber and complacency? It is time to fast and pray and weep for the nation. God says to us through Joel 2:12, "Return to me with all your heart with fasting and weeping."

Jeremiah advised us, "Let us examine our ways and test them, and let us return to the Lord. Let us lift up our heart and our hands to God in heaven and say: 'We have sinned and rebelled and you have not forgiven'" (Lamentations 3:42).

But if we return to Him we can be confident of His forgiveness because "He is a forgiving God, gracious, compassionate, slow to anger and abounding in love" (Nehemiah 9:17). Jeremiah said, "Because of the Lord's great love we are not consumed for His compassions never fail. They are new every morning; great is His faithfulness" (Lamentations 3:22-23).

As the Bride of Jesus, let us renew our first love to our Savior and ask God to make the book of Acts come alive in our churches. Why was the early church so powerful? Why did the Holy Spirit move among them so mightily? Why were they able to heal the sick, see wonders and miraculous signs and have the Lord add to their number daily? And why were so many being saved? Because they devoted themselves to corporate prayer. Whether they met in houses or in synagogues, they made themselves a house of prayer. As they prayed, the Spirit of God moved continually and powerfully among them.

Where are the corporate prayer groups among believers today?

Oh, may the Holy Spirit move mightily in our churches so that our neighbors may see the fire of the Spirit. May they run to us and ask how to be saved. Oh, may we be like the New Testament Christians!

Let us continue to cry out to God for our younger generations to seek first the kingdom of God. Let us ask God to raise them up and prepare them for the battle to win this nation back to God.

Oh, young people, this calling is for you. How big is your burden? God is calling you to embrace His burden for the world, especially to win this nation back to God. Are you willing, young people? Teenagers? Are you willing to yield yourself to God for this purpose? You are the future of America. You win it or lose it.

My question to all of us: How big is your burden for the younger generation? Just as Jesus wept over Israel, just as Jeremiah wept over his nation, will you weep for America?

Let us be humble before the Lord and repent for ourselves, our families, our churches; repent for our nation and for all nations around us.

Jesus wept over Israel. Jeremiah wept over his nation. When was the last time you wept for America? Jesus pleads with us today, "Will you help me bear My burden?"

CHAPTER 5

Will You Repent with Me?

"O Father in heaven, You have declared to us through the prophet Jeremiah that we, as a nation, Your people, have committed two sins (Jeremiah 2:13).

"We have forsaken You, the Fountain of Living Water; we have dug our own cisterns that cannot hold water. Therefore, Father, we have witnessed the curse on our land.

"Yes, we are covered with shame. But, Father, here we are in Your presence as Your people who are called by Your name. We humble ourselves before You, we pray, we seek Your face, we repent, turning from our wicked way. Will You hear us from heaven? Will You forgive our sins? Will You heal our land?

"We hear Your Words through the prophet Isaiah. '...though in anger I struck you, in favor I will show you compassion' (60:10).

"Thank You, Father. 'For You are a forgiving God, gracious, compassionate, slow to anger and abounding in love' (Nehemiah 9:17). We pray in the name of the Lamb of God who has taken away our sin. Amen."

CHAPTER 6

The Dream that Intensified My Burden

About four years ago, I sensed God was leading me to leave a large home church to join a small congregation located in a mall. As I walked the mall, I prayed for each person I saw inside and outside the stores. Sometimes I stopped and talked with them, and at other times I prayed with them if they allowed me.

I found my heart "enlarge" (Isaiah 54:2) with the Lord's pain for the lost. That's when He gave me this dream.

I found myself riding on a scooter in a community that looked totally black. Everything was black like charcoal or soot or tar, including the people. They also looked skinny and dry. People were wandering in the streets, moving slowly. Some were still and looked lifeless without a purpose.

They were mostly young people holding big brushes in their hands, and they kept painting themselves with tar.

I was perplexed and wondered why I was there. I wanted to get away from this horrible community. But I got more and more lost.

Suddenly, someone jumped on my scooter and twisted my arm. I almost screamed…then I woke up, touched my left arm and realized it was only a dream.

I wanted to forget the dream. I thought, "It is so unpleasant to keep in mind. It's not attractive for anyone to hear." But I thought God might have a message in the dream, so I asked Him for the dream's interpretation. I remembered that most dreams in the Bible are unpleasant, but they always have a message. In Ezekiel 37 the prophet had to look upon a heap of dry bones.

Because of the predominance of the color "black" in the dream, I decided to research the word "black" in a concordance. I discovered the following:

"The punishment of my people is greater than that of Sodom, which was overthrown in a moment without a hand turned to help her. Their princes were brighter than snow and whiter than milk, their bodies more ruddy than rubies, their appearance like lapis lazuli. But now they are blacker than soot; they are not recognized in the streets. Their skin has shriveled on their bones; it has become as dry as a stick. Those killed by the sword are better off than those who die of famine; racked with hunger, they waste away for lack of food from the field" (Lamentations 4:6-9).

Verse 8 has similar descriptions to what took place in my dream. Verse 9 says the people looked black because they suffered starvation from a famine.

Then I read Amos 8:11-12. "'The days are coming,' declares the Sovereign LORD, 'when I will send a famine through the land —not a famine of food or a thirst for water, but a famine of hearing the words of the LORD. People will stagger from sea to sea and wander from north to east, searching for the word of the LORD, but they will not find it.'"

Famine is a judgment of God upon a nation. The commentary footnotes in my Bible say, "The most horrible expression of God's wrath comes when He withholds His Word from His people." This is far worse than a tsunami, a flood, an earthquake or a war. Lamentations 4:9 states, "It's better to be killed by the sword than die of famine."

Revelation 6 talks about seven seals, and the first four seals mention four kinds of horses. Each horse represents destruction upon the earth.

"When the Lamb opened the third seal, I heard the third living creature say, 'Come.' I looked, and there before me was a black horse. Its rider was holding a pair of scales in his hand. Then I heard what sounded like a voice among the four living creatures saying, 'Two pounds of wheat for a day's wages, and six pounds of barley for a day's wages, and do not damage the oil and the wine'" (vss. 5-6).

In these two verses, the third horse is "black" and represents a famine. There seems to be a connection in Lamentations, Amos and Revelation in regards to the words "black" and "famine."

This dream may be a picture of our nation right now. Our nation may be suffering from a famine of hearing the Word of Life.

The Word has been faithfully preached Sunday after Sunday in churches and also at retreats and in Bible studies everywhere. Seminars and conferences are increasing in every corner of the nation, yet our nation keeps sinking in deep darkness, in blackness. It keeps drowning further in deep immorality.

Even though we hear good reports of salvations within our churches, it seems on a small scale in comparison to what we hear from the rest of the world. We are receiving many reports of how unbelievers are coming to Christ in China, India, Africa, and other nations. Luis Palau was in Vietnam, and about 3,000 Vietnamese accepted Christ in that communist country. Even Muslims are turning to Jesus.

Paul says in 2 Corinthians 4:4, "The god of this age has blinded their minds so that they cannot see the light of the gospel that displays the of glory of Christ, who is the image of God."

But now, I'm convinced that God Himself has shut their ears from hearing the living words—the Word that breathes life upon the dry bones, the Word that brings light into darkness, which displays the blackness of a nation.

Our nation now seems to be an open wound for the enemy since God's wrath withholds His Word from people whom He formed for His glory.

Peter and Jude (2 Peter 2:17 and Jude 13) echo the same for the ungodly, for those without the light on their path.

"These people are springs without water and mists driven by a storm. Blackest darkness is reserved for them" (2 Peter 2:17).

"They are wild waves of the sea, foaming up their shame; wandering stars, for whom blackest darkness has been reserved forever" (Jude 13).

Reading through the book of Lamentations, lamenting along with the prophet Jeremiah, I also saw a glimpse of Jesus, agonizing over Jerusalem. "The days will come when your enemies . . .will encircle you and hem you on every side; they will dash you to the ground, you and your children within your walls" (Luke 19:41-44).

I saw a glimpse of Jesus struggling in the garden, drinking the cup—the cup of wrath, the cup of fury in my place. I remembered how the disciples were so unconcerned.

Then God highlighted Lamentations 1:11-12. "All her people groan as they search for bread; they barter their treasures for food to keep themselves alive. 'Look, LORD, and consider, for I am despised.' 'Is it nothing to you, all you who pass by? Look around and see. Is any suffering like my suffering that was inflicted on me, that the LORD brought on me in the day of his fierce anger?'"

I then recalled what I saw on TV a few days prior to the dream. First, there was a 16-year-old student who was killed by his friend because they both wanted the same girl. Next, there was a 20-year-old mother who killed her baby. And finally, it was reported that a man had raped a 92-year-old lady. I shut the TV off and went on with my routine...perhaps I had grown used to hearing these things.

But later that day, a voice came from within with a gentle rebuke, "Is it nothing to you, Nancy? This is My burden, and you tried to ignore it."

I realized then why God led me to this dream—so that my eyes would see exactly how God sees this nation—a nation in the midst of a horrible famine of hearing the Word of Light, the Word of Life.

When God sends a calamity as a judgment on a nation, He Himself is in deep distress, in deep anguish. Here is how Isaiah describes God's emotion in Isaiah 42:44: "like a woman in childbirth, I cry out, I gasp, I pant." At the same time, He looks for someone who will bear His burden so that He does not have to destroy the nation.

Ezekiel 22:30 states that God looked for a man who would build up the wall and stand in the gap before Him on behalf of the land so He would not have to destroy it, but He found none.

Isaiah also said, "He saw that there was no one; he was appalled that there was no one to intervene" (59:16). God constantly looks for intercessors. Throughout history, we see that He would not move without intercessors.

When David sinned against God, God sent a plague to kill 70,000 men. But when David built an altar to sacrifice the burnt offering to the Lord, the plague stopped. "Then the Lord answered the prayer in behalf of the land and the plague was stopped" (2 Samuel 24:25).

What a mystery. What a compassionate God.

If Aaron and David could stop the plagues of God's wrath on behalf of their land, you and I can call on the Name of the Lord on behalf of America to stop God's wrath from our nation.

The night of my dream, I had gone to bed about midnight with a burden of the Lord that I didn't choose to bear but with a hope that God would raise up more intercessors to pray like men in the Bible. However, our hope is not based on our intercession but on God's character and His compassion. "But you are a forgiving God, gracious and compassionate, slow to anger, and abounding in love" (Nehemiah 9:17).

On another occasion the word came to me, "There is a famine of hearing the Word of God in this nation." I cried to God until I exhausted myself, asking Him how to remove this famine. God woke me up around 3 a.m. I expected His words to come to me, and this is what He said, "You cannot remove their famine of hearing the Word of God by increasing your effort in teaching and preaching the Word. This famine can only be removed by My own Hands. My faithful followers must come to Me, in my presence like Moses came in the burning bush. I will work through your earnest and believing prayers along with a broken heart." I knew "a broken heart," meant having a broken heart— broken as Jesus had been broken for each of us. It's as if we enter into the very suffering of Christ with self-denial.

"I lift up my eyes to you, to you who sit enthroned in heaven. As the eyes of slaves look to the hand of their master, as the eyes of a female slave look to the hand of her mistress, so our eyes look to the Lord our God, till he shows us his mercy.

"Have mercy on us, Lord, have mercy on us, for we have endured no end of contempt.
We have endured no end of ridicule from the arrogant, of contempt from the proud" (Psalm 123).

CHAPTER 7

For Such a Time as This

The revivalist Leonard Ravenhill saw the spiraling downfall of this nation, and in 1979, he wrote the book *America Is too Young to Die.*" He is right. That time has come. We are, as a nation, at the point of death. Yes, we are dying as a nation!

I'm one of the millions from a poor and an oppressed nation who came to America to find refuge because I heard that God blessed America more than any other nation on earth. But now, where can the needy nations find such refuge?

Today you and I are witnessing that all government programs—including the entire economy—are close to bankruptcy. The moral life of our nation is collapsing! Even God's church has failed to be salt and light to preserve and to protect the land. Many churches today are dry and weary. Some are even dead! God commanded us to be set apart to rescue the nations, to revive the church, to carry out the Great Commission. Unless we pray and allow God to revive us as a church, there is no hope to bring this nation back to life.

God needs a Mordecai and an Esther "for such a time as this" (Esther 4:14). God does not need a famous preacher like Jonah who was full of self-focus and wanted to serve God in His own way.

How did Mordecai rescue God's people? When Mordecai learned that the king had ordered all the Jews to be destroyed, he became severely burdened. (Esther 4:1) He tore his clothes and put on sackcloth and ashes—a sign of sadness and repentance. He went out into the city wailing loudly and bitterly as far as the king's gate to burden all the Jews. Has God placed a similar burden on you for this nation?

As it was in the days of Mordecai and Esther, revival begins with a burden! There was great mourning among the Jews with fasting, weeping and wailing in sackcloth and ashes. (Esther 4:3) When Queen Esther heard the news, she, too, became burdened and deeply distressed. Mordecai sent a messenger to Esther urging her to "go to the king's presence to beg for mercy and plead with him" for the sake of her people. (Esther 4:8) Esther realized she was the only hope for her people who were at the point of death! Could it be that the future of this nation also rests upon you?

As it was in the days of Mordecai and Esther, those in the remnant (those saved by grace) are the only hope for our nation and for the world for such a time as this! If we don't do as Mordecai and Esther did, we can't expect others to do it. We cannot be complacent like Jonah!

Mordecai said to Esther, "Who knows but that you have come to your royal position for such a time as this?" (Esther 4:14). Esther took this burden seriously upon herself! All of the Jews fasted for her. She and her maids also fasted three days without food or water. Esther said, "When this is done, I will go to the king, even though it is against the law. And if I perish, I perish" (Esther 4:16).

With courage and confidence, Esther went to the court of the king. "When he saw Queen Esther standing in the court, he was pleased with her and held out to her the gold scepter that was in his hand. So Esther approached and touched the tip of the scepter" (Esther 5:2).

Oh, what a moment! A moment that forever changed history!

The beauty of Esther attracted the king so much that he forgot she had broken the law! That is how attractive we are to be in the sight of God when pleading for our nation. The lover in Song of Songs exclaimed toward His beloved: "You are altogether beautiful, my darling; there is no flaw in you. You have stolen my heart, my sister, my bride" (Song of Solomon 4:7, 9).

When God looks at us that is how He feels about us when we are sharing His burden! Oh, the Blood of Jesus! It's because of the spotless Lamb of God who "suffered outside the city gate to make the people holy through His own blood" (Hebrews 13:12) that we can be God's beautiful, holy bride!

The king then asked Queen Esther, "What is your request? Even up to half the kingdom, it will be given you" (Esther 5:3). If you read through the story, you will find Esther got much more than half the kingdom.

Jesus, our King, says a similar thing to us: "And I will do whatever you ask in my name, so that the Father may be glorified in the Son. You may ask me for anything in my name, and I will do it" (John 14:13-14). Note Jesus' passion for His Father, "Ask whatever you want in my name so that I may bring glory to my Father"! The glory of the Father must be our passion, our aim, and the end of our prayer.

As it was up to Esther to present her request before the king, so it is up to us to approach our King. And Queen Esther's request was granted!

After Esther's first request was granted however, "Esther again pleaded with the king, falling at his feet and weeping because her people were still doomed to destruction. She begged the king to put an end to the evil plan of Haman the Agagite, which he had devised against the Jews" (Esther 8:3). It was critical for Esther to ask the king to put an end *to the evil plan* of Haman so that the enemy would have no more power over the Jews.

Again the king granted her wish by allowing the Jews to protect themselves so that they could put an end to the enemies and devices just as Esther had asked of him. (Esther 8:11) The power of the enemy needed to be completely destroyed.

When God commanded Israel to conquer Jericho, Joshua then commanded the people, "Jericho and everything in it must be completely destroyed as an offering to the LORD" (Joshua 6:17 NLT). In verse 21, the people obeyed and completely destroyed everything in Jericho.

God also commands us today to put an end to all evil thoughts and evil deeds among us, the body of Christ, because these are the enemies of our souls. (I Peter 2:11) The enemies of our soul must be completely destroyed. Our life must be an offering, a living sacrifice—pure and holy unto the Lord. (Romans 12:1)

We, the holy bride of Jesus, should be as Esther was to the king—so attractive that God accepts our ongoing petitions for our nation just as the king accepted Esther's earnest requests. Do you have the spirit of desperation like Esther had for the sake of her people? Have you wept before God with your request for our nation? Would you be willing to put an end to anything in your own life that is not pleasing to God for the sake of the nation?

This story reveals many glorious results through the efforts of Mordecai and Esther. It was more than they ever could have dreamed because of the way God worked through Mordecai and Esther:

• Haman, the enemy, was destroyed by the very method he had planned for Mordecai's death. (Esther 7:9, 10)

• "When Mordecai left the king's presence, he was wearing royal garments of blue and white, a large crown of gold and a purple robe of fine linen" (Esther 8:15).

• "In every province and in every city to which the edict of the king came, there was joy and gladness among the Jews, with feasting and celebrating. And many people of other nationalities became Jews because fear of the Jews had seized them" (Esther 8:17).

• The tables were turned on the enemy, and the Jews got the upper hand over those who hated them. The power of the enemy was destroyed! (Esther 9:1, 2)

• "No one could stand against [the Jews], because the people of all the other nationalities were afraid of them" (Esther 9:2). "Mordecai was prominent in the palace; his reputation spread throughout the provinces, and he became more and more powerful" (Esther 9:4).

• The queen continued to find favor in the eyes of the king. The king asked Esther, "But now, what more do you want? It will be granted to you; tell me and I will do it" (Esther 9:12 NLT).

• Esther received everything she asked for. Plus, Mordecai became second in rank to the king and was held in high esteem by the Jews. (Esther 10:3 NLT)

How did Mordecai and Esther reach these wildest dreams? It was through God that

1. With a spirit of remorse and in sackcloth and ashes, Mordecai humbly called them and mobilized them to join him in crying out with a spirit of desperation for the nation.

2. Esther went to the king. She could not afford to wait for an open door or wait for a chance to be called by the king but boldly went before the king. She did this at the risk of her own life—all for the sake of her people.

3. With great courage and leadership, Mordecai and Esther motivated the Jews to be united.

Power comes from uniting minds and hearts in prayer. As in this story, God only needs to call one person who is willing to carry the burden of the Lord. He can use that one obedient person to burden others until united prayers become desperate and powerful enough to move the hand of God.

Let us then go into the inner court of *the* King, standing with confidence before God, to beg for mercy and plead for our nation until we touch the tip of the gold scepter and hear Jesus say, "You can ask for anything in my name, and I will do it, so that the Son can bring glory to the Father" (John 14:13 NLT).

Let us humble ourselves like Mordecai and Esther until we cry out with Esther: "How can I bear to see the disaster fall on my people? How can I bear to see the destruction of my family?" (Esther 8:6). This has been my daily prayer for years.

As stated earlier, our nation is very close to bankruptcy in every way. I agree with Anne Graham Lotz: "Babies are not only aborted but sold piece by piece on the market. Sex trafficking is thriving. Marriage has been redefined. Nations are unraveling. Wars are raging. Arms deals are being struck behind closed doors of our enemies" *(www.annegrahamlotz.org/events/911-recall-to-pray-for-jerusalem/)*.

Besides all this, I continually receive prayer requests from individuals directly or indirectly crying out to be set free from the bondages of pornography and some from homosexuality. I echo Queen Esther and cry along frequently, "How can I bear to see the disaster fall on my people? How can I bear to see the destruction of my family?" (Esther 8:6).

Looking into the near future of our nation, I am greatly burdened for our younger generation. Are you? Do the young people know how to face all that is about to come upon their lives? Do they know how to face the battles of the present conditions in our society?

Mordecai and Esther were the only hope for their desperate people. We are the only hope not only for our nation but also for the vulnerable younger generation!

I urge you to begin a prayer group or join an existing group in your church. Mobilize corporate prayer where you work or in your neighborhood. God is calling us to fast and pray, not just pray. Let us cry out for the future of the nation to our Father, who is the "forgiving God, gracious and compassionate, slow to anger and abounding in love" (Nehemiah 9:17). Oh, how the next generation of this nation so desperately needs to be rescued from the hand of the enemies!

And with confidence, in the Name of Jesus, let us plead with God to revive His church and to revive America "For such a time as this," whatever the cost! It is time to obey. Is God calling *you* to step out for such a time as this?

CHAPTER 8

What Will You Do with This Message?

1. Mordecai became burdened—and shared that burden with Esther. Together Mordecai and Esther became burden-bearers that resulted in taking action—even to the point of risking their own lives. Are you willing to take on the burden for your nation?

2. Esther not only fasted, but the people also fasted. Are you willing to fast so that your nation and family will not be destroyed? Will you encourage others to join you?

3. When is the last time you made sure your inner beauty was so pure and radiant that as you approached the King of kings with passion for your lost nation, He welcomed you and listened to your plea as you claimed His promise "ask anything in my name, and I will do it."

4. What glorious results could come if you, like Mordecai and Esther, are willing to intercede on behalf of your nation?

5. Could the glorious results be more than you have ever dreamed? Would those wildest dreams include—

a. You humbly going before God with a spirit of repentance, burdened for God's people to the point of calling them, mobilizing them to join in crying out with a spirit of desperation?

b. You going before the King of kings, even if it means risking your life, to plead for the freedom (from sin) for your nation?

c. You pleading and petitioning with united minds and hearts in prayer with other Christians for the spiritual revival of your nation?

d. You going into the inner court of the King, standing clean and with confidence before God to plead for our nation until you hear our King Jesus say, "You can ask for anything in my name, and I will do it, so that the Son can bring glory to the Father" (John 14:13 NLT).

6. What is your daily prayer? What if you are the only hope for the desperate people of this nation? Will you join me "for such a time as this"?

ACallToAmerica.org

Order multiple copies of this book

Subscribe to Aletha Hinthorn's blog

www.ingramcontent.com/pod-product-compliance
Lightning Source LLC
Chambersburg PA
CBHW060557030426
42337CB00019B/3566